RED, YELLOW, BLUE

STICKER AND DRAW

This edition published by Parragon Books Ltd in 2016
and distributed by

Parragon Inc.
440 Park Avenue South, 13th Floor
New York, NY 10016
www.parragon.com

Written by Susan Fairbrother
Illustrated by Abi Hall and Ruby Taylor
Consultant checked by Geraldine Taylor
Edited by Laura Baker
Designed by Karissa Santos and Clare Phillips
Production by Charlene Vaughan

ISBN 978-1-4723-9210-7

Printed in China

RED, YELLOW, BLUE

Note:
To get the best learning out of this book, it is recommended that an adult work alongside the child.

PaRragon

Bath · New York · Cologne · Melbourne · Delhi
Hong Kong · Shenzhen · Singapore

Sticker the clouds from light to dark ...

Light gray cloud.

Fluffy **white** cloud.

Little **black** clouds,
ready to rain!

Big **dark gray** cloud.

Take cover!

The sun shines light and
the clouds pour rain.
Together, what do they make?

red

orange

yellow

green

blue

indigo

violet

A rainbow!

Color it in.

Red truck, **yellow** truck, **red** truck, **yellow** truck,

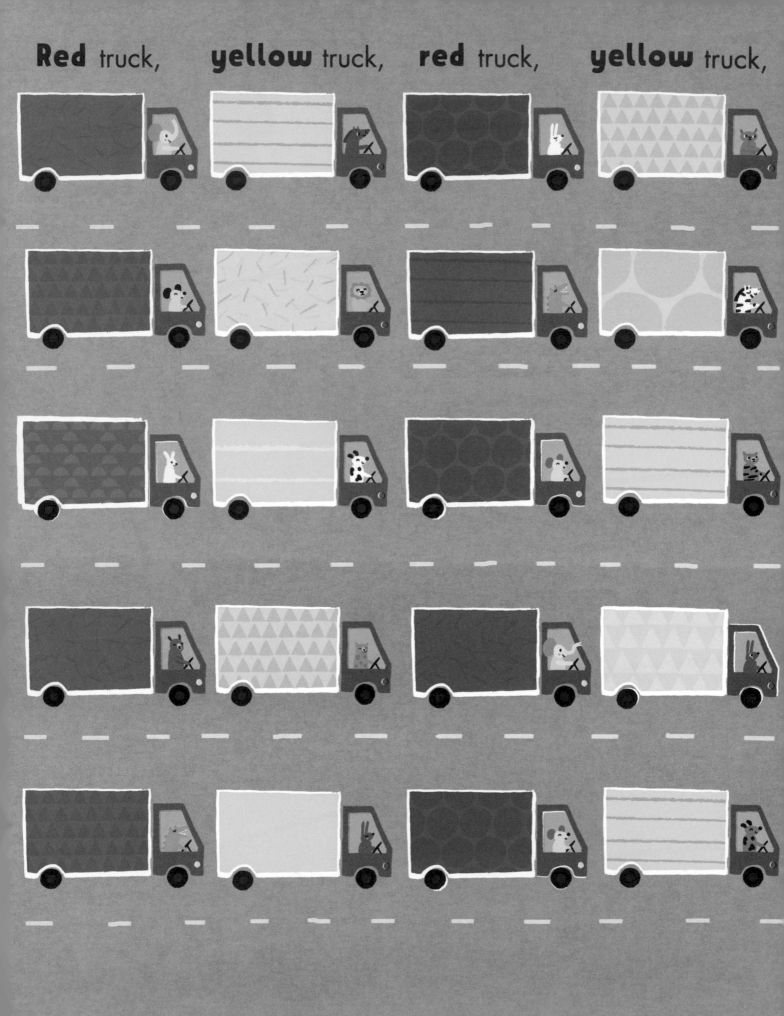

red truck, **yellow** truck, **red** truck, **yellow** truck.

Circle the odd one out.
Finish the patterns in black below.

Sticker 1 **red** dot,

2 **yellow** dots,

3 **blue** dots,

4 **green** dots,

5 **orange** dots,

6 **purple** dots,

7 **black** dots ...

Now color more and more dots!

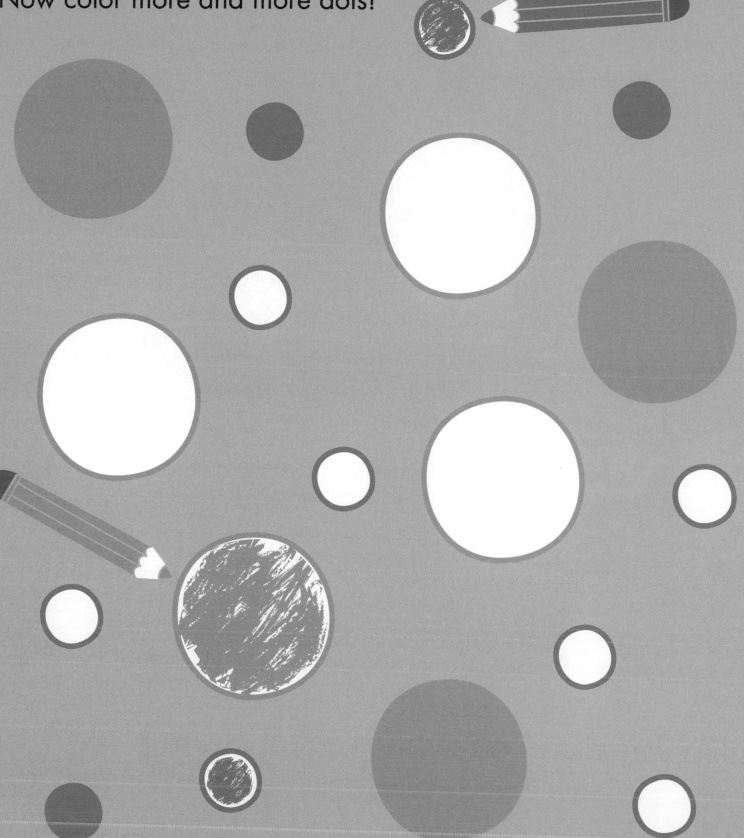

Make the **big** dots **green** and the **small** dots **pink**.

White sheep …

Change the white wool to black. Now they're all …

There are three main colors.
We call them **primary colors**.
Point to each color and say its name.

RED

YELLOW

BLUE

Sticker in more things
to match each color.

Arr!

Captain Yellowpeg loves anything **yellow**!
Circle 10 **yellow** things.

Here are Captain Redmane and Captain Bluebeard, too! Circle something **blue** and something **red** for each of them.

Answer:

Mixing **red** and **blue** makes ... **purple!**

red + blue = purple

Mixing **blue** and **yellow** makes ... **green**!

blue + yellow = green

Mixing **red** and **yellow** makes ... **orange**!

red + yellow = orange

Stick on some **purple** things.

Stick on some **green** things.

Stick on some **orange** things.

Let's add a little **red** to **white**...

+

=

It's **pink**! You've made a **tint**.

Sticker in tints of pink, going from light to dark.

LIGHTER

DARKER

What if we add a little **black** to **white**?
It's a **shade**!

+ = This shade
is **gray**.

Stick gray jigsaw puzzle pieces to
complete the picture. Color some pink in
the elephants' ears!

We're ready to land!
Stick planes at the matching color airports.

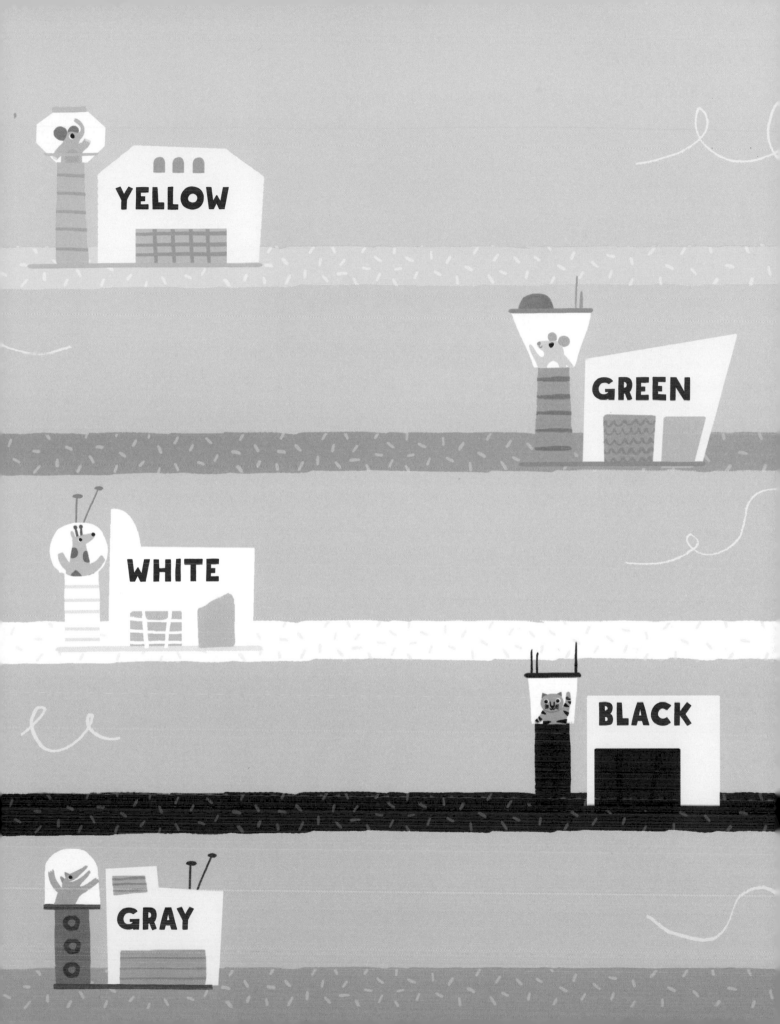

What a lovely landscape!

Now go color crazy! Color the sky **purple** and the grass **pink**. Sticker a **yellow** cloud, **blue** horses, and a **green** sun.

Who's hiding where?
Write the number in the box.

Green frog

Blue bird

Blue octopus

Orange cat

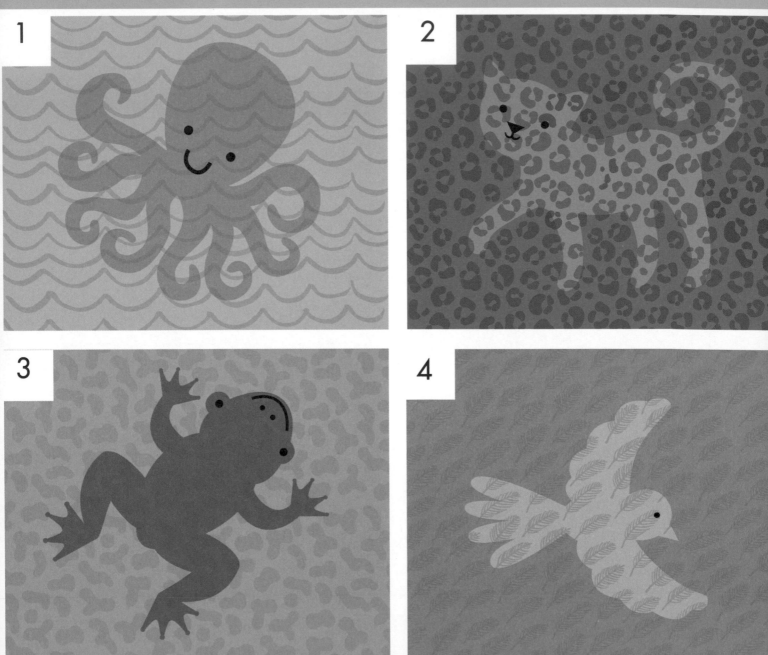

Zebra, Giraffe, Peacock, and Snake want to hide, too!
Stick each one on its matching colored pattern.

These are **warm** colors.

What is your favorite warm color?
Draw something in that color here.

These are **cool** colors.

What is your favorite cool color?
Draw something in that color here.

Brr, it's chilly here! Adding a little white to blue makes an icy tint.

+ =

Color the sea **dark blue**.

Color the ice **icy blue**.

Stick a big
blue whale.

Sparkle and shine!
Jewel colors are deep, sparkling colors.
They are named after precious stones.

Draw lines to match each crown to its jewel name.

ruby

emerald

sapphire

amber

amethyst

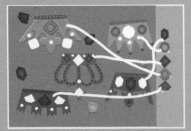

Answer:

Cover the crowns
with matching
sparkling jewel
stickers.

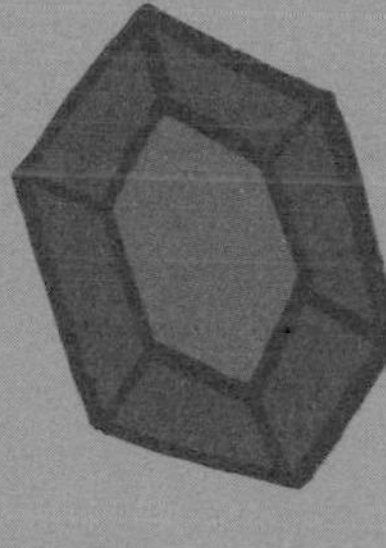

Who lives in the dark, dark cave?

Press hard with a crayon or pencil to make it really dark in this cave.

purple

light brown

blue

dark brown

green

Spooky! Stick on lots of eyes in the dark.

The aliens are ready
to blast off!

Navy Blue

Sea Green

Chocolate Brown

Lemon Yellow

Coral Pink

Crimson

Trace the lines to take each rocket to its matching planet.

Warm Summer

Stick on warm summer things and cool winter things.

Cool Winter

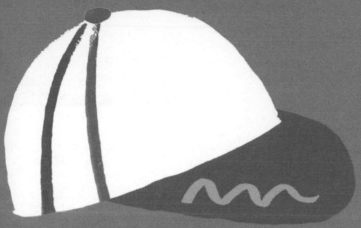

All in **orange**!

pink and **purple**

Doodle in color to complete these patterns.

blue and **green**

shades of **blue**

red and **yellow**

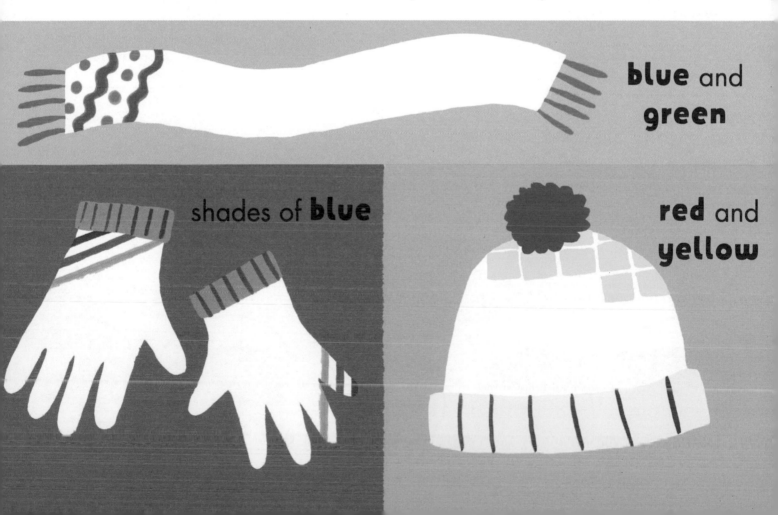

Pick a paint pot sticker.
Doodle a picture using
shades of this color.

Now pick and stick
another color.
Doodle a picture using
shades of this color.

Color all the shadows **black**.

Stick each missing **green** cactus in place.

When the sun sets, the sky fills with warm colors. Color it in pinks and oranges!

Now color the trees and animals in a dark color to stand out against the bright sunset.

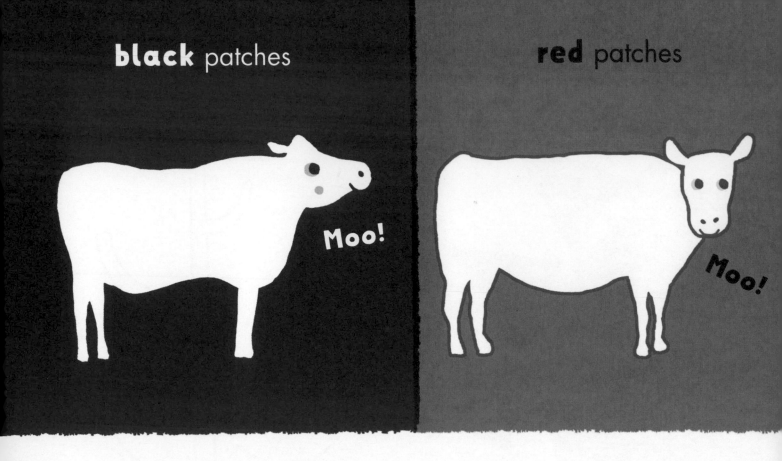

black patches

red patches

Moo!

Moo!

Add matching colored sticker patches to each cow.

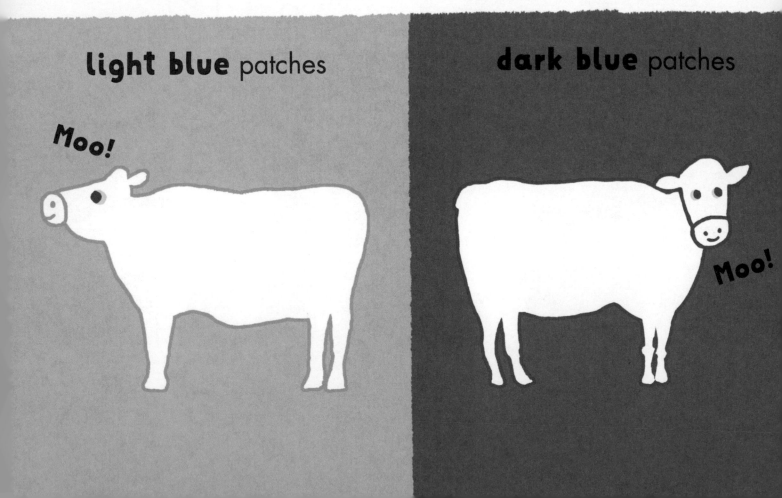

light blue patches

dark blue patches

Moo!

Moo!

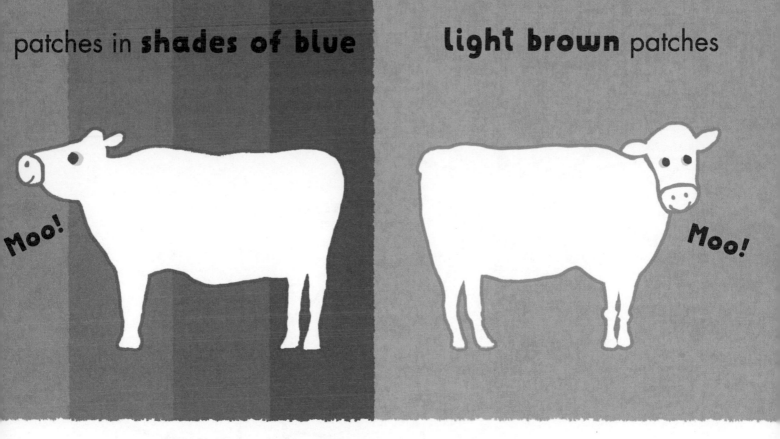

patches in **shades of blue** light brown patches

What crazy colors!

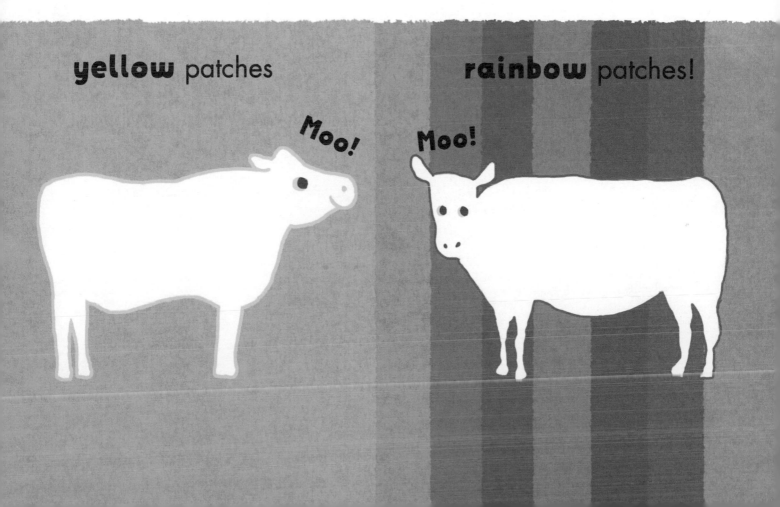

yellow patches **rainbow** patches!

Color the flowers!

blue

orange

red

indigo

violet

yellow

green